THE RIGHT
TAXI

WILLIAM J. REWAK

A Book of Poems

ISBN: 1475187483
ISBN 13: 9781475187489

Library of Congress Control Number: 2012906808

CreateSpace, North Charleston, SC

To the Memory of my Parents,

WILL and ELDORA

CONTENTS

PART II

PROLOGUE

IMP

We toss and play with words, string them
out, admire their elasticity and thereby
paint for ourselves a halo of authority,
create a voice
         to be heard;

Chaucer knew that and he wasn't
trying to be humble in a Christian way
or obsequious in a self-serving way:
he gathered up his stories
held them in the palm of his hands
and weighed them against his heart:
which would spring him into grace?

And look: Prospero wiping out
all the beauty he had conjured
because he had found his rest.

We spend hours spinning words
(have we even advanced from the rhymes
         of giants?)

to enlighten and please in a pygmy way

but it doesn't take us closer
it doesn't crumble the distance
it's not the penance we feel born into
nor is it the hard, embarrassing genuflection
we're called to.

But – the imp in us says, "Spin."

PART I

THAT AFFABLE FAMILIAR GHOST
WHICH NIGHTLY GULLS HIM WITH INTELLIGENCE.

William Shakespeare, Sonnet 86

THE LOONS

Rufus rode often
with his grandmother out onto the lake
where loons played and complained
through the night; though small, he plied
the oars well – he knew this
because her eyes told him so.
She recited from all the classics,
teaching him how to orate
with the rhythm of his arms: "O,"
she'd cry, "I have ta'en too little
care of this." And other words.
He stacked them up like waves
in his mind and they rolled in his dreams:
long sentences with ripples
in the middle, short phrases
that pounded his heart with her inflection
(stark, lonely, as if it were caught
surprised in a crater of the moon);
she washed words so they'd shine.
The loons followed her and when she spoke
they circled in silence.

EBONY GRACE

She peers around the door, wary
of imposing: grey curly head
with ebony grace. She sees minutes
passing, too fast, reaches out
to halt them, punctuate her wish.
Time was, everyone marched
slowly under the hot sun and she
parsed with care for her charges:
a blackboard washed with chalk spelt
lessons too hard for some to learn,
but she pushed, and words began to grow,
pictures flamed; she knew where
to plant. Now, long past
those humid days wiped clean
with thin cotton, she limps in
and waits to be heard. Her eyes,
heavy with old light, ask
that the room pause, take note;
she cannot impart in a moment the violent
ignorance she has bloodied, the rage for those
who turned and stumbled into long ditches,
the loud joy she sang when a sharp,
tight bole broke into blossom.
She waits. As when a conductor
lifts his baton the silence builds,
the chattering now stops, strings
stretch unheard, waiting for the bow:
the hot sun shines through walls
of glass and she again begins to parse.

FATHER'S DAY

You turn with a question toward the whisper
the pine branch makes on the window
and then place before me a pad and pen
and say in case I need it there it is:

you do not say what course of thought
impels this offer. In your darkness
do you hope I'll write my soul
so you'll know what to say next

time I visit? It's hard for you to sit
and trade words; but that was always
true, you had looked at me and hoped
I'd hear what you couldn't say, then you'd

throw a punch in jest to teach me
what I refused to learn. These words
you want me to write now: would they translate
better than the silent ones before?

You had other sentences to arrange in your
tool shed, that fine prehistoric dictionary
whose puzzling alphabet only you understood;
but from those tools you fashioned our lives

and I thought God could not have done worse
if he had used the same for his own work.
I will entrust them now to archives
and pray for time to decipher them.

Cold footsteps in the hall remind us;
the pine branch is still. Perhaps
this is what keeps you here: waiting
for me to use the pad and pen.

GARDEN

She flounces in, carrying yet one
more vase, this one filled

with daffodils; a soldier, she arranges
her ammunition and secures unattended areas -

there's a dead spot right near
the bookcase, needs a bit of shoring up -

yellow should go well with the white roses
on the mantel and blue periwinkles on the coffee

table, which look across the room at calla
lilies standing proudly in an urn

near the door; there are violets and camellias,
baby's breath and, she thinks, what did I

miss? no, everything's set.
She has invited Nature to invade her salon

to combat the coughing that disrupts the silent
air; if the colors are properly mixed,

strewn about according to plan, then all
will be well; here and there a petal

falls, but they can be silently swept away; now,
with curtains opened, sunshine can break in.

FIELDS OF CORN

He sat and pulled taffy out of his mind
tugging and twisting but it wouldn't snap
free; so he closed that part of the day
and hailed a taxi, hoping that a wild ride
down Park Avenue would polish his attitude,
one he was not proud of but nevertheless provided
a fur-coat feeling he could use
when dealing with the very tall presidents
of the slick companies operating in the moon-
touched steel of everyone's idea
of the perfect skyline. He joyed with New York,
whether it simmered in tar or sprung
like ice stalagmites against a slate sky;
he did not need the divine,
this fumbling little man
with the red bow tie, he discovered
he did not need anything
more miraculous than a cold sun
(Apollo greeting starved fields
of corn). He threw a bill and jumped
out of the taxi, skinned a beggar's plea,
resolved to improve, and burst into his bar.
Voices covered him in green mist,
lawns spread to the sea, O'Dooley's
sang of gold; but he dismissed such
ravings - though he liked to be reminded -
drank his third, and whistled on home.

HOMECOMING

You walked in lost, hair touched
by evening mist, light from candles
made you a rainbow - there you were
smiling so full of gladness

you had arrived but a little late
we were ready to hold you long, still
you stood dazed unable to believe
your journey over, the past healed

cries of dark winds pushed
away in caves buried in years
owls free now to dip
through the night, you watch them

and see the spirit of all you lost
but here now a press of love
I wanted to jump on your rainbow
and slide down with joy into your heart

to brush away the warped shadows
of ashen crossbeams to prove you were
right: mountains can be laid low
streams will jump and dance again.

BLOOD ON HIS GLOVES

My squirrel sat on the tip of a sawed-off cross of a tree
each morning, chomping on little buds to keep his tummy full

and I noticed his tail: squirrels have graceful, full tails:
God's gift, to make the rodent an appealing creature

one can write poems about and take pictures of on rocky slopes
in Colorado even though they run rampant at home - but this tail

was wilted and sparse as if too many years of chomping
had passed and he was headed for the last round-up;

my father's hair was sparse at the end - natural, of course -
but he had lost the diligence of my squirrel: no climbing

the uppermost reaches; the boxing ring where he fought
when young and always raised a fist before he found

an opening, the blood on his gloves, all this he resented;
a slung hammock now his home, but here the constant

between the two: darting eyes that searched reasons
and would not back down: one troubled a tired twig

the other the conundrum of death: how far could each bite
into their subject and remain sure of the answer; my father

closed his eyes at the end with teeth still clenched
as if trying to force even the stars to speak or wondering,

finally, how to say there had been love; my squirrel
kept chomping until, one day, he fell to the ground.

JUDE

Jude was a serious man:
he learned spelunking
so he could travel the deepest
dark where only the non-sparkle

of a bat'e eye cast a shadow;
he'd crawl for miles, whistling
show tunes to keep critters
happy and obliging; he wanted

to find the secret of darkness,
uncover its source, wrap it
tightly and bring it to the light
so it would vanish, but each time

he thought he had touched it
it melted away and moved
farther into the deep; Jude
never quit on a job, so if

you hear under your feet a soft
sound of music or an old-time
lullaby of Broadway
you'll know he's on his quest.

ENCYCLOPEDIA

I used to be afraid to touch
the ground here, the grass
crisp and alive, shadowed

by blocks of granite, but I wander
now, less like a visitor,
and note the smooth rusting

of names and dates; sounds
have grown softer, no empty
screeching, bluebells in the corner

give comfort. Yesterday,
the gardener mowed and lined
edges, making everyone

secure, their roofs neat
for colloquy; and in the sun I swing
my arms and stretch my legs

(the end of a run) and wonder
why we paint this scene
in crows and empty branches

for here, now, lies
an encyclopedia of love and hope,
a place to learn what others

suffer to know. The attempt
goes on outside the gates
but - the rest is here.

DECISIONS

I want to get the details down right:
she's standing, I'm told, on the edge
of a cliff, her sight skipping over
the massive ham-fisted rocks that

strut their way down toward Big Sur,
she's impressed, apparently, but still
wondering why the continent stops
here and not farther out, though happy

about the steep drop: she unties her
scarf and lets it blow billowing down
watching it catch at the air; they've
described her that way often and I'm

trying to get the colors right because
tone is important in a crisis, you want
to bring a soft brown in here and there
to balance the more aggressive reds

and greens, this one is going to be different,
it will speak of mystery - we're partial
to that - but there will be a homespun quality
to her stance, too, to take the edge off things.

A PIECE OF RAG

I found, once,
a piece of rag
marking a page
in a family Bible;
on the rag
was written in red,
"This is the place."
Since that day,
I've envied the ghost's
hard certainty.
But did he keep it?
Now, has he planted
a new place,
with proper dimensions
and sequential pagination,
has he read through
and made a choice,
decided when to stop
and what to skip?
Can he put his finger
on one moment
and dispense with the rest?
Or does he wish now,
with half a turn
and half a look,
for a torn rag
with red markings?

JEREMIAH ON WALL STREET

Bellowing and roaring
you march into my office
carrying your own private
brass band in your throat
to denounce the chaos
of our world and point
to so few rainbows and
how even they have grown
pale; I will sit stitched
and wait for the band
to wheeze itself out
then I will say that while
most in your circle would
look to Eden, I look to
Abraham for taking things
so seriously and to Moses
for disrupting well-organized
plans and to Jesus for being
such a stickler: discords,
all three of them;
they could not abide
the ancient harmony
flowing from mountaintops
the cloud-wrapped notes
that kept us free;
you it is who are chaos

smashing your way
through an order we have
sedulously resurrected;
so soften the decibels,
doff your scarf and move
to warmer climes.

GREEN CHARTREUSE

"Of all the gin joints
in the world. . . ,"
and there she was,
my own refugee,

sipping green chartreuse
and discoursing on Aristotle
(her heart opened
for dead philosophers,

mainly because
they were dead)
holding court
for eyes that wanted

more than Aristotle
but were willing
to walk the plank
of matter and form

for a dip into cleavage;
and I stood by watching
pulling pencils
keys and coins

out of my pockets
to arrange an intelligible
life to attract her
but the clinking of the coins

broke the scene
and I was left to wonder
if matter is more
ethereal than we had supposed.

THE ORCHID

I placed an orchid by her bedside while she slept
and tried to remember where I bought it – not

necessary to know but the steps I've taken lately
have grown blind spots and I want to isolate them,

unpackage them, so that unfogged I care for her needs:
she's the broken one, slipping in and out of rooms

she always carefully carved from light, and I had thought
I'd last in order to guide her through them, holding secure

in my hand the map we drew together; but if the map
is shadowed, how shall she and I know where to go?

LA SEÑORA

The steps down were the most fearful, but she entered
the clanging train each morning, ankles full of water,

and tried to gulp down the day as if it were her last;
she pondered again the morning's words: "we shall all

be changed, changed utterly": hope dropped
into her hands: listening, Rodrigo's notes, bursting

from his darkness, sang in her heart: she was born
for Valencia, not this stinging dustbin of chewed gum

and urine, the left-overs of moles whose ride is a flight
into shadows. She wanted a royal mantilla and a sun

she'd gallop with down to the sea: bones to combat
chance, ankles to fit and arms bathed in cream;

then she'd lift her new voice in praise of the saints
and kneel at the high bell: cloisters would arch

her beauty; the sky would open and soft dust swirl
around her feet to glint the day. The train slowed

as she lifted her packages and walked out again
where she could not run and searched the passage

for a herald she prayed was there but could not hear.

JACOB

I agreed and went down to Laguna to watch him die;
405 to the toll exit, turn right and left a few times,

up a hill, and I'm on the porch; I stood and looked
at the door knob for a while and remembered how

with his three-fingered hand he always wrestled with it
to get in, then stomp the floor as if to announce an ogre;

he was like that: there seemed no placid bones in his body
and when he had an idea - instead of coaxing it carefully

he'd grab and twist so that often he'd just spew out mush,
and we didn't like the taste of that so some walked away;

I wanted to break his arm so he'd see the problem
but I doubt that would have made a difference

and I'd have regretted it, especially now; we were, after all,
only acquaintances who grew up in the same room and this visit

was a presumption he and I often traded, trying to find
our way to one another through detours and stop lights;

his words came slowly, spilling out onto a cashmere blanket
and draining away, their tentative odor all I can remember

of them; his one eye bulged and nearly spoke itself
but then closed also; a glass of water stood half-full,

some pills had been scattered; he was done wrestling for now.

SIR GAWAIN AT HOME

He would come in after midnight and set aside
his spear, armor and chain mail doublet,

sit and wait comfortably for his martini
before reviewing the day and the battles:

dragons were the most obstreperous, often
declining to be beheaded, even offering a bouquet

of dandelions as a bribe for freedom, but he was
above bribes and always took the matter in hand,

not without a small prayer of thanksgiving
for the occasion; as he sipped, and the logs crackled

he still harbored regrets that life on a broad highway
had been left behind, that he was set on a course

of dank pathways shadowed by forests he often
found puzzling because noises were muffled

and the sweet undergrowth of wild roses, ferns
and yellow crocuses belied the horror he knew

marched quietly beside him as he moved according
to the plan he had devised so long ago; the sun shone

somewhere.

JUSTICE

They hanged him there
in the courtyard for all to see
a mere bud at the end of the rope

petals tight

those staring saw only twitching
while bright blue towered
with no lightning

the land around was watchful
birds sat with wings folded
against the light

they were not afraid
they lifted their baggage
hustled the children away

as the street emptied
a dust-devil danced

and God reached down
to water him

that was a while ago

it is a field of yellow now.

AUNT CHRISTINE

While this is not what I would have chosen
I'll eat it anyway: Aunt Christine says we are a race
with few choices: hummingbirds and spiders
are a given, the sun rises and sets; the young
speed their years and the old lie waiting;

so anything presented on a plate by creation
is worthy of attention.   On another planet,
I would concur, but my slippery mind,
also presented to me without my request,
prefers to discern different steps on

the ladder of creation, to judge that blooming
roses are more aromatic than their roots,
that imagination can travel faster than snails,
Caravaggio's lines have more depth
than my stick drawings – that my soul hungers

in a way my toe cannot feel. Aunt Christine
gets lost easily: I have confounded the fence
she has built around her life, the small acre
she knows so well: years earlier, someone
opened the gate for her; she slipped and fell

along the hillside; now she cooks my meals
brushes her skirts and sticks to the wisdom
of her enclosure. I am not ungrateful, so
I lean over and fork with regret the turnips
I wish, in her acre of content, she'd stop planting.

THE DAY

You said you wanted to die on a bright day
so you could find your way clearly to the shore;
you said noon would have no distracting shadows
to maneuver around, for you believed the lore

that the soul is haunted by them; you said the day
should be long because you never could walk fast
and you wanted not to be late; but here you are,
stretched out in dark winter, betrayed, long past

the summer's light; but is there ever, finally, a day
perfect for what you now know? Does our world
prepare us correctly, with its colors and its din,
for the moment we all shun when we are hurled

into silence? You do not speak. No matter the day,
then, no matter the silver clouds from the west:
you've packed away your trinkets and lie with empty
hands, ready for what someone else knows is best.

THE BASEBALL TICKET

He was the one-eyed giant when we were young
handing out baseball tickets because he thought

that's what made us strong and I, burrowed into
Dickens, could not understand his predilection but

his kindness overrode any gravel I felt in my mind
and I clapped my hands, a twelve-year-old tyro,

so he'd know I loved him and understood his wish
to give us happiness; his last baseball ticket I found

in my desk and so though I didn't see the game
I hold it close and remember his one eye winking.

POETRY

They shut him away in a cage
where food and drink were supplied

but no mentor to teach the empty days
no candle to befriend the night

so he wove together sentences
        hoping
they'd provide a key to open his cage

and let him walk freely.

PLAYFUL

Outside my door, ghosts are walking
up and down the sidewalk, turning

diaphanous heads to glance in every
once in a while to see if I am still

watching because they like attention
and also want to disabuse their more

grounded cousins of the legend
that they are here to frighten us;

rather, they are as playful as any child
who has escaped a playpen to travel

around a room and discover corners
it can get lost in; as playful as any bunny

that has found an open door. I keep
watching because I want to learn

beforehand the route I will travel
and the attitude I will certainly adopt.

THE BUBBLE

For Max, it started with a small tickle in the back
down on the right side, then a quick stab one morning

as he was ladling oatmeal which was always the get-up-and-go
he needed for the rush the day would bring; at noon,

while juggling right and wrong, a full spasm from neck to knee
made him sit and forgo contemplation to zero in on pain:

the world of thought receded and his back took precedence.
As the day trudged on, Max stepped inside a bubble, painted

it black on the inside and allowed words no entrance; he heard
a chattering of echoes but knew they could not understand

the world he now occupied: the lightning that clawed him
and the deep emptiness of reason that gave way to unreason,

the clanging troop of horses galloping around his soul at will.
If he could reach the pinnacle of pain, he could plot his course,

but it seemed always beyond where he stood; he was dragged
further than he could ever have guessed and knew, finally,

the crucifixion of desire, the last step we take.

WONDER

It is impossible to clean my room
without disturbing the dust
of lost conversations and forgotten
          appointments;
it is impossible to walk a hallway
without finding footprints
that tell a song I sang
          once
when the air was quiet, when
doors did not slam shut;
it is impossible to sit on the sand
without imagining castles
or a laugh that lasted longer
than the explosions that fired the sky;

all these are dredged
to no purpose, except for wonder.

HE WAITED

He lay in his grave and heard faint voices
from above, then clumps of dirt, he supposed,

on the cover of his coffin; he wanted
to say, careful there, it's expensive oak

(at least they told him it would be)
but he wondered mostly about the next

step and how he was to extricate himself
in order to take it; he preferred light

to darkness, he told the priest, so he
presumed they had arranged it for him.

He took dips in the valley during his life
but they were for recreational purposes,

nothing serious, nothing to concern God
(who had bigger fish to fry), so he relaxed

took stock of a contented life, and waited.

BUT, LUDWIG

"Music will change the world"
(Beethoven)

Beethoven journeyed toward deafness
along an avenue of music,
willing to duel with the knife inside
so he could scold chaos;
"My song," he told us, "will design
your souls." He could be heard
in the small rented rooms of his pilgrimage,
pounding keys in white thunder,
stamping his pattern for change.

But, Ludwig, all these centuries
of the harp, the violin and horn
and not a variation in the world's rhythm?
Still discordant in conversation?
Would you now, in hindsight,
and with all your senses at full speed,
throw out your four pianos
and find comfort in carpentry?
Which testament would you choose:
a solid chair without hope
or the Ninth in ordered self-delusion?

SUNT LACRIMAE RERUM

You sit there in a corner
two inches from the TV
to pick up on the political
palaver, no eyesight,
ears barely hearing
the arguments, but I marvel
at your persistence
and anger, that something
outside of you - outside
of your brokenness -
can capture your imagination
and make it jump over hills
make it boil

there were moments
when the wind off the lake
blew open doors
and cleaned the whole house
but you stood hard
and held the walls
then the moon would rise
silver would break
the dark corners
and the house would sleep

the gardens now are soft
your lilacs
gave off their last scent

how will we know
to care for you?

ROADRUNNER

"It's a bright and guilty world."
Michael O'Hara in "The Lady from Shanghai"

Only a child thinks forever:
having learned of no other possibilities
in the few years the three of them sat
hunched together for the evening news -
with a flip to the Roadrunner during commercials -
she presumed the conversation would continue;
she remembered, early on, the bustle
on oatmeal mornings, riding high
on her swing out by the long green beans,
and laughing as words made sense.
Sunshine was heavy then, burrowing
into the earth and exploding into sunflowers,
sweetpeas and blue larkspur - the blossoms
she'd pick and arrange around her day;
afterwards, she scattered the dried petals
as sacramental leavings of a finished task.
But she thought things human remained
(as she thought bones would always be straight):
then, without careful parsing, one went
one way, the other another,
and the evening news continued its digression;
mornings were quiet. She objected
she had not been prepared, that swings and beans
were no lesson, the sun should have hinted
at a colder language. You don't hear
whispers on a swing, she learned; you miss
eyes looking into the distance when the Roadrunner

has you riveted, wondering if once again
he'll evade doom. You don't notice
hands not touching and you don't know
about the black space when words fail.

BEETLE

Martha was one of many as she marched
down the boulevard carrying placards

denouncing wrongdoing of every sort
because she was always against wrongdoing

and lifted her fists in concert with all oppressed

but once at night she heard a thunderclap
so she pulled on her shoes to investigate

and found a land bereft of all trees
a soil denuded and streams bottled up;

while she stood in wonder, a beetle moved
in close and asked if she was the savior

they'd been expecting but she answered
politely she was only one of the singers

in the choir, so he bowed (as best he could)
and teetered away, while she wondered

if she spoke too soon.

FAST FORWARD

Willie watched others' lives
speeding by as he sat, entranced,
in one old cattle car
after another; he flicked cigar ashes
at the jumbled screen of accidents and mistakes,
cheered the tricks small boys
played on their sisters, watched with a pang
of memory as a young woman left
by a back door. Enough imagination
remained that after years of travel
he'd often blink and turn away,
shamed he could not confer absolution:
"But I see more than most," he'd say,
"and if the world cannot find grace,
it lies content knowing it is observed."
Willie rode on; his ears
are clouded now from the loud snap
of the rails and his eyes see only
shadows: trees are pillars of black
that mar the landscape and hands that reach
are puzzles of bone he cannot decipher;
his fast-forward life has confused
perspective. If he cannot bless,
he can wait, pity the images
he feels flying by, pray for the stop
he knows was scheduled long ago.

PEARL WHITE

She's the kind who dreams of being Pearl White
because deep inside she knows lightning can dart
from her fingertips and spread salvation, she knows
she can bend to the imprisoned and quietly impart

a love that brushes the air she breathes or fearlessly
take on the perils of an onrushing locomotive;
each night as she kneels she imagines embracing
a city, a nation, the world, then lights her votive

lamp in humility, knowing distress is too vast a field,
too ingrained to be touched. Though - a call is a call:
so she continues to dream of derring-do far beyond
her space, but walks in courage, twitching her shawl

like a latter-day prophet, greeting clowns and killers
and the desperate as if they mattered, as if each soul,
mired or winged, is itself a pearl to be snatched, cleansed,
sparkled, and with panache, made whole.

PART II

A MAN SHOULD EVER, AS MUCH AS IN HIM LIETH, BE
READY BOOTED TO TAKE HIS JOURNEY.

Michel de Montaigne, *Essays*

ABUNDANCE

See this piece
of crystal
how the light
fractures?

It's the fracturing
of beauty
so there is more
to go around

to admire.
The earth opens
each day
that way

each time
a deer leaps
each time
you smile.

COMFORT

I want to reach out and say,
"Don't worry, the pain will find
a new avenue and then it will leave.
It has many places yet to visit."
I want to touch you and brush away
the cobweb: "No spider stays for long."
But is any of that true?
Pain doesn't travel, it multiplies;
and spiders still move to a prehistoric chant.
What is true, and what alone I have,
is a hesitant hand that has flinched
at pain before but is still, admittedly,
a novice. Take it. At least it's warm.

A DAILY GAME OF SOLITAIRE

I won again! This silly game
distracts me from more beneficial
pursuits, but the challenge

of mastering the odds has been
my journey and I see this game
as a way to prove the odds

can be beat. Shakespeare did it
every time he penned a line,
Caravaggio did it every time

he touched a blank canvas,
and every saint does it
as the last bell is rung.

At first, the odds are daunting:
it's the gift of existence we do not
choose, but we open it and proceed

as directed; if followed carefully
we can puzzle our way into
all the secrets of alignment;

then we, too, can become saints.

WAITING

I awake, lie there, rise and sit on the edge of the bed,
wait for muscles to get the message, stand, move slowly,
step by inch - or: put my foot into a sock, it's tight,

my toenail spears a thread, take it off and try again -
or: spread the sheets, fluff the pillows, then wait
for cold water to turn hot for shaving, wait for coffee

to boil: that's just a few, but – oh – the time it takes,
the minutes spent on useless minutes, the lack
of an Aristotelian motive, the wasted breaths Melville

could have easily filled; what hours can I count in a day
that tax the brain or fluff the heart? We squeeze them
in between and around the dallying, the waiting in offices

watching people waiting, in lines at the bank watching
people perplexed and bored, waiting; and what about
those waiting for the Parousia? Meanwhile canvases wait

for paint, paper waits for script, Twain waits to be read
and Hopper to be gazed upon, and loved. Perhaps that's it:
love has lost its force; otherwise, we'd pump the morning,

show Hopper to those who wait and invite everyone
to drop their socks and shaving cream for a golden ride
in a raft down a joyous Mississippi. Yes! we would.

CHALLENGES

I have derived my life
from small events:
the apple I eat
each morning,
the twigs I sweep
away, the stair
I daily climb,
the sighs I try,
with prayer, to decipher;
these are challenges
we do not ordinarily
meet with fortitude,
we demand more
for our courage. But
since a child
I have listened to the prophets
who have warned us
we should not ignore
our daily bread.

JUMBLE!

I'm caught in a jumble
a forest of crackling leaves
branches swing with a screech
crows are squawking
falls roar into the deep
and bears crunch their way
with loud yawns
and unsparing tread

jackhammers readying the land
and locomotives blaring
across midnight

I've been taught
to turn aside
and deepen silence

there's the rub

the stridency of all
that is good

how do we dig down
listen to the music
that was planted
crack the code

and accept the lilting joy?

NOW AT DAWN

A bird flies past
my window

a thought across
my spirit

I live in a place
birds love

so I get
many thoughts:

they're quick
evanescent

untamed
so do not linger

I hear the rush
and run to capture

but it's no use
perhaps they're better

left to the wind.

THE LESSON OF PYTHAGORAS

Wait and see, they keep telling me,
sure that's easy for them to say

sitting there in the bleachers while
I'm down here in the arena with net

and spear to ward off the lions
and even those pesky squirrels;

wait and see, life will change,
soon you'll be on your surfboard

marrying waves, they yell,
but all I can hear is a roar;

how joyous it was, so long ago,
to struggle through the Pythagorean

theorem and clinch for myself
the innate order of his vision.

Those beautiful lines on paper?
I've never found a good translation.

CHINESE VASE

It was easy, sitting on a beach,
toes in hot sand, to see

all the way to the rim
and to know the rim is only

a curve, but now feet are shod,
the briefcase is full, years

have been scraped away
and distance gets lost.

Is it because we've eaten
the dinners we took such pains

to prepare, fondled the Chinese
vase we no longer travel to see?

This, I know, is the ruse we let in
and once in our living room

it gets comfortable, drawing
shades and marking out narrow

parameters we learn to accept.
It's necessary, then, to escape

to where the light falls from above
where gardenias on red lacquer

romp with egrets in flight.

INQUIRY

I dusted
    carefully
fixed meticulously
my Windsor knot
noted eyes
    watching
and wondered, "Am
I in the right zoo?"

AWAKENING

I put on a yellow sweater this morning
because I wanted to feel alive, I wanted

to stand up and compete with the dawn
to spread the yellow gift down all the way

through to the smallest gnat and tell
the dull grays and browns that color

is on the way, that a garden, once forsaken,
is going to ripple with life, that petals

of forgotten hues will unfold and twigs
will stretch their fingers into the light:

a gate, once barred, will swing open its arms
and invite all prayers, all hopes, and all pain.

LISTEN

Listen, quietly, for words
which must fight their way

through smog to get on the board
words that speak the things

we cannot say aloud
for they rend a conscience

but words that are truth
because they come from

deep in the earth, passion-filled,
where life begins outside dogma

where life fights its way
to the surface with its own music

and will not change the notes
will not turn for the penny offered.

RUCKUS

They're all downstairs having
       a party
and I'm up here trying
to make words;
there's a cement floor
between us but I hear
       the laughter
and the clinking of glasses
and I wonder if heaven
has to put up with the ruckus
       we create
if the noise
is sometimes too great
if it disrupts their serenity
or if like glorious oak trees
they look down and embrace
the confusion.

INTERVALS

Each morning I spread the peanut butter
evenly and to the corners or, on another day,

ensure the syrup is contained between two slices
of French toast. I am derided for my orderliness -

often bending to the dropped pennies of our day -
but we all have ways of getting through the world

because we have to compensate for the intervals,
the moments when chaos sneaks in and the program

crumbles: when evening arrives and images flutter,
silk falls across the arm, or when rage is unlocked

because it has grown too big for its cage, when even
a sad glance at blossoming wisteria fails to work -

when prayer seems stunted and love is brusque.
The intervals remind us we have a way to go

but they are not therefore ready money,
casually accepted and freely spent, gifts to use

because they are there or, worse, a light
break, easily absolved because we turn again

to even corners. They exist because we walk our lives
in time, which offers a variety of options, at different

speeds and whimsical allures; we cannot always maintain
the itinerary we work out for ourselves in better times.

PEAK

My grandmother who spouts wisdom
like spittle says pears have a ten-minute
peak so you have to sniff carefully

touch lovingly to discern
that window and I've thought her wisdom
should not be wasted on pears

(though she also has a line about prunes
and belly buttons) because it's the peak
we all work to, walking up the hills

till we reach the moment we're flush;
after that we get soft, don't we?
However, I've discovered the peak

that's always reachable, never conquered
and piles itself on itself so one
ten-minutes is a small thing, just

a step. I've discovered a conversation
that doubles and triples, bursts
into a rose garden where gnarled

wood finds fertility
hidden and life is always
one peak more.

PERSPECTIVE

The mountains to the north are light this morning
non-obtrusive, a child could run them up and down;

they flash red and orange in the sun with azaleas
and poppies; but all is at a distance. Closer, like fears

that move in to stay, they harbor caves and deep mulch
where a soul can be lost and never retrieved, pathways

end at a drop, trees become an Oz forest and we are at
a loss to find the light that seemed so obvious

when we sat in armchairs ten miles away sipping
gin and tonics and discussing the rules of perspective.

GUARDIAN AT KING'S CROSS

a black porter stands
by my door as the train pulls out,
"would you like something,
    sir?"
and I am not aware of any need
just perhaps a small wish
to sit and watch the fields
    wave by
        with their white sheep,
pieces of cotton strewn
    over rich green,
"no, thank you," and he bows slightly
and leaves, his right elbow
stuck out as if leading
someone away,
    his knees jerk, too,
and I am happy he is here,
    he is real,
the book I've brought is half-done
but no nearer its argument, filled with facts:
number of artillery units necessary for
a swift engagement, rounds of ammunition
available, the air strikes needed for effective
control:
and I don't want to get to the end
    so I ring the bell
        and ask the porter for coffee
close the book, and when he comes
ask him if in his kindness
he would lead me away.

MIX

I watched the moon
this evening
     rise
over the Golden Gate
stretch its white
     over gold:
a neat partnership
when girders can dance
     in God's light
when the deep blue's
blend of space
and our home-grown
candles wash
     our eyes
with May;
each beauty
we hold is a frail
     mix
of the earth's garden
and our play.

"LA BOHÈME"

They're singing to beat the band
"La Bohème" coming out all
beef and whipped cream:

bravado, poverty and wine
but soft - hear how its melodies
dip, chasing a violin;

they rush to close the veins
of the soul, belie the Aristotelian
calm; if Mimi can so enter

and disrupt with her final plea
where can peace be found?
Her notes sting as I walk

to class; how shall I lie
about the knife at my throat?
It is terror we learn from love.

THE PEG

Each morning after a breakfast walk
I hang my sweater on a peg in the closet,

knowing it will be safe until I need
it again, because the peg is rooted

in a hidden beam that stretches from the cellar
to the roof, a sturdy tree that will hold

branches of other beams, plaster boards
and leaf-green wallpaper, portraits

of the past - and my favorite peg: I need
such strength for my peg, it must

be available for the worries I entrust to it before bed
and humble enough to bear cast-offs.

It's the one sure thing for the day,
like another's shot of brandy or someone

else's morning prayer; we depend
on such gear for their connection to the beam.

ENOUGH!

You know how you get when you want something
more substantial, there's an itch under the fingernails
you feel the eruption coming, volcanoes are used to it

but the heart has a hard time with sudden movement,
it can be love or that deeper one jealousy, then as sudden
the rains come and wash all the exciting parts away,

but that is our fix, and it goes all the way back to Adam
and his lovely who were not quite sure how much
they had inherited. Enough! Blame is easy, fact is

my heart limps; I'd like to have it otherwise,
but here is one advantage: all the frozen clutter in there
has been spoken for, I offered it up one morning at a wide

gold-encrusted altar like some tyro who didn't have
a clue but who was ready for dragons; how do we
predict the dragons are mealy-mouthed gnats who

require more than swords to slay. Enough! Begin with
love, trust in that eruption and then laugh at your
ancestors' portraits. They're all cross-eyed, anyway.

THE CAT STARTS SCRATCHING

Young, the desire is not there:
no evil intent, or even
rudeness; the heart is not baked enough
to want the final touch; the brain
has no antecedents to know the lack.
What seemed piety, for most of us,
was either a need to please or a halting
attempt to discipline grace. Like
disciplining a cat. If peer
followed peer into the darkness and named
it light, there was, at least, company
and therefore corroboration. But two eggs
every morning, for years, you want
more. Some parts die
and they tug, not forgotten; some
start pulsing, urging, unready.
And the cats starts scratching; the light
is still darkness but it beckons, insistent,
then you know and desire finds its way.

JOURNEY

It was a Vermont landscape:
red and gold zigzagged
through the trees
and a clean white spire
made assertions of its own.

Far to the left, beyond
checkerboard streets,
in an unruly expanse
of deserted farmland,
a scarecrow stood

in benediction - upright
and firm, waiting
for a slick intruder.
No Oz scarecrow,
but one with eyes

that recalled the first
sacrifice.
Music moved in
with autumn,
troubling the chaos;

quickly, to prevent
his smile, I shot
the scarecrow and,
quite unaccountably,
he bled.

BELIEF

When I was young enough to believe,
we would wander through the old lot that snuggled up
against our house on the left; on the right
stood our orchard of apple and cherry trees,
an Eden of possibilities for the naive and hungry,
but on the left was mystery and, perhaps, revelation;
three great maples shaded
a timely riot of small discoveries:
blackberry bushes rooted and tangled
underneath lilacs, and under blackberries
grew wild strawberries, while up through
strawberries sprouted, each year,
early crocuses with their Easter colors
that initiated the summer canvas; soon,
here and there, in breathless clumps,
white lilies of the valley dropped
their sweet fragrance and thereby fastened
memory to a time and place. Bluebells
began, then wild roses
sprang out of vines and blushed as they climbed
the maples. Out of holes hidden
from long before our parents arrived
to claim the land, crawled mice,
gophers and green garters (but much
down there remained hidden).

We spent truant hours watching
this work, heeding woodpeckers and crickets,
sampling the fruit that ripened around us.
We did not understand attribution,
but the brushwork was impeccable; even the sky,
pale hot blue or exploding
with dark thunder, functioned as a backdrop
for the riot, and for those so young.
In such a way did the world fashion
our home and make it strong dogma.

PRACTICE

After all the conversation
about dreams and petty preferences,
after the cocktails and near
attractions to preposterous personalities,
after calendar fights
and the soothing of deformed hearts,
what remains of value
is a lone boat on a lake
that mirrors a white
house on a lonely shore.
With one figure
standing guard.
This is not, my friend,
a tragedy; it is what
we come to, and I'm enjoying the practice.

OUR DAYS

You and I have spent our days scratching for light
and I assumed that when finally our hands lay

at peace, the fabled dawn would make all clear
and all the efforts played out on side roads

would be seen in place, the dust would shine
on green willows; but I'm here now and the only

advantage is a clarity of dark, my only message
a puzzle that still needs centuries of prayer to resolve.

FINALLY

I want a simple sentence
that reflects the life
      I live now
what went before is a paragraph
with metaphors and dependent clauses
semi-colons, dashes
      and italics
but a noun verb and object
      in that order
suits me fine as I sit on a bluff
watching the sun order its day
listening for the music
of a single violin.

PART III

BUSY, BUSY, AND EVER BUSY,
I DANCE UP AND DOWN TILL I AM DIZZY.
I CAN FIND FANTASIES WHERE NONE IS. . . .

John Skelton, "Magnificence"

TIME OUT

They noticed that the sun, in setting,
wedged itself between two sentinel trees
and couldn't budge. Since they
were not ready, they smiled at the opportunity
and moved down the street,
scuffing golden leaves, to say goodbye.
Long shadows bent around white walls
and painted a '52 Ford resting on
carefully arranged piles of brick;
a laugh broke through a bedroom window.
Red bougainvillea blossoms
tumbled across the pavement
promising a more lush return,
while Mrs. McLaughlin's water sprinkler worked
overtime on two corner rose bushes.
Danny and Joe wrestled on the front lawn,
ignoring pleas of "Bedtime."
"Not yet. Not dark yet."
Further along the street, they turned:
the voices were winding down
(but more slowly - even the streetlights,
following the City Council's schedule,
were clearly confused by the stranger light).
This was important: grass that needed cutting;
a fire hydrant that needed paint;
Mr. Larcher's front porch that needed support.
Was it the need that made them last?
And, then, the sun slipped through.

MARMATHYN THE WHALE

Marmathyn the whale was content to flip his tail
and send spouts of water to the sun in delight,

he sounded well and full, then rushed up again
and burst into an air of wide horizons, free to laugh,

to wonder about the line where sea climbs the sky
or how the wind, like him, can somersault the world;

and when great gales came he'd thrash the waves
to show them who's boss; though he hardly ever prayed.

One night a black deluge flipped him (he thought
of his birth and of how bright the sea then was,

how sparkles in a great blue tickled him, and he wished
he was there again when music seemed endless

and the smile that nuzzled him blessed him) -
and as he opened his mouth to cry for help

a clump of kelp plummeted in and ran along inside.
And then he prayed. He prayed

for three days in pain, looking for his sparkles in the blue,
begging the whale-god for a return to birth

so he could swim another way. In the quiet lingering
west of light he coughed, blinked, and took off

for a quieter sea; each night he'd pause in thanksgiving
but would never know he had saved a king and a city

and a simple man who had himself been in the throes of birth.

THIS SAD RACCOON

Drowned he was, this sad raccoon,
in rain that never stopped; he waddled
through mud and brushed past drooping

ferns, did not pause
when errant streams swept by.
He didn't notice. Lightning only

darkened his step. He pondered a smaller
world of storms that had more
bite: she had said, finally, no.

Creatures not familiar with raccoons
may doubt their ability to love only
because they have never talked to one,

but if you untie the knot of language
that snarled from some primitive misunderstanding,
you will hear sounds slip into syllables

that spell words, and from those halting
dictionaries a grammar that structures the heart.
Eyes tell, then, more

hunger than we are used to in such pets;
paws lift in appeal and brows
squinch in consternation; a walk is rude

or inviting. This one, here,
choking through his storm,
may not use the logic of our sounds,

but he glories in his own government,
and he can tear any dream we build
or any poem we presume to write.

SCORPIONS AT PLAY

In a small Baja village
scorpions at play hop over
      a page
of Elizabethan script
      (a Jesuit
in the seventeenth century, weary
of baptisms and death, had saved
some candlelight each
      night
to wander through greener lands);
one scorpion stops,
reads of Falstaff's babbling,
then stings himself.

DRACULA

"Time is a pregnant elephant," said
the owl, "motherly, but terrifying. I look
back over my own years
which started sometime during Dracula's
first intimations he had a problem
and I can say - without prejudice
to my family - that our vaunted wisdom
has been a publicity stunt dreamed up
by planet-crazed poets searching
for symbols to arrange their own chaos."
"Well," squeaked the mouse, settling in,
"you've dumped time and myth and symbol
into one fairly presumptuous statement.
Furthermore, I cannot agree: time is a pretty
little thing we hold in our paws
and must be petted with grace or it becomes
petulant and flies away to someone else."
The owl blinked: "You don't know it
well enough to speak of it; it sits a stone
on the heart. The centuries I know are marbles
we fling across the void: a dash of color,
no more." The mouse sat quietly;
for fear of seeming ungrateful, he did not
want to preach to a higher being,
to point out that when you have only
one potato chip, the bag
looks attractive. But he did have a question:
"What has Dracula's penchant for blood
to do with wisdom?" "Pull your chair
closer," answered the owl, "and I'll show you."

MODERN WARFARE

A cockroach clicks
across my floor
sniffing for grease
I lie bulky
      bedridden
defenseless but for a boot
wait! I cannot
accuse it of martial
      invasion
its intentions are benign
its heart an empty
shell of dark
      yet
any advance
on my person
must be countered
with appropriate
      severity
nations protect
their beaches
kings hold
fast their jewels
cannot I therefore
      save
my bacon?

THE SQUIRREL

The squirrel sits on the back
of the chair, tail twitching,
attention is set and he's ready
   to go
then he jumps on the lawn
runs circles, spies
a mate and chases (branches
are avenues, not obstacles) -
   then stops
      and listens
hops back to the chair
once more at attention:
he has a deeper purpose there
his soul squeezed tight puzzling
but the little squirrel mind
   gets lost,
acorns sex and frolicking
get the better of him;
if he would hold his head
   still
for a moment - but then
he wouldn't be a squirrel.

DISCREET

He sits with soup and a British thriller
alone, in a quiet St. Ives hotel

and while Mrs. Dawson is being butchered
he cannot help but hear another operation

whispered, and sees a hand brushed aside
but he turns it off, back to fiction

easier to concentrate on logic written
than illogic spoken; he follows the scent

then catches the steak beurre blanc
arriving at their table and they pause politely

he turns the page quickly, is this true?
They toast with red wine, she slams, sloshes

it on the table, hisses words never meant
and he's following his own words

mysteries have a puzzle of emotion often
difficult to grasp but he's content to know

solutions, now they rise and his hand moves
so slightly, the noise wakens them all

and when she falls he wishes he had not registered
in a "smart, stylish, and discreet hotel

near the water, known for its tranquility,"
because he's lost the line that separated

his table from theirs.

PORCUPINE

I weep for you, Porcupine, because I cannot see how
you have many friends; we are used to touch and taste
and smell but with you there can only be a far glimpse;

you sit alone in your den and read the exploits of others
trying to decipher the avenues of bravery you have not trod
(or waddled) and wondering, as you watch television,

if there is not some part, a prickly one to be sure,
that you could play and be believable as a leading man;
you've emailed your kinfolk for advice, but they, too,

sit and wonder if, by chance, they've been forgotten,
or mis-made, if they never were dwellers in Eden
but arrived after, with other natural catastrophes;

so you sigh and keep the sweet world at bay and know
that what you have heard whispered about the lunge of love
can be no more than a moment's screech in the long night,

and you beseech the God who arranged that all should be,
who exploded the earth with a million geometries of light,
to bend down to smooth your plight, and hold you close.

WHISPER AT NOON

If you look deep down
into the heart of a diamond,
you'll see a speck of unrest:

it's struggling to shine;
for all of its glory, it itches
to achieve the one dazzling

stone in all the universe
that can never be repeated,
the one flower that will send

its aroma to the farthest galaxy
and be honored for the task.
There are other things

we need to know if we are
to survive: why redwoods
can be cut but never tamed,

how oceans feed us, why God
steps around us gingerly
and sculpts our facets with precision

why evening light recalls
a death. We plunge into reality
at birth and begin:

there are lilacs along the road
fireflies at night
a whisper at noon.

THE EGRET

An egret stepped warily into the trattoria
on the corner and ordered a pasta with marinara;
the clientele paused as one pauses
when cocktail chatter is broken by a belch
or as happened the previous evening when a rhinoceros
waddled in for a martini: it was getting increasingly
difficult to eat without the odd interruption.
The owner (a Neapolitan) was open-minded:
he believed meals have a spiritual flavor
relished by all of God's kingdom,
that a table is the communal center of creation.
But his diners refused to countenance feathers
and snorts, to extend their fellowship to those
considered less favored in the chain of being.
Rumors spread about his tasteless predilection.
He lost business. The egret, though,
a snowy delight in his dark day,
chattered on about marketing, new customers,
seasoned opportunities, a unique vision
in an expanding world of gustation.
The Neapolitan - who first saw light
at the edge of a vast uncornered sea -
stood in the night and watched
the still stars, so far away.
They stayed bright, no matter
the turning of the world. He nodded,
returned to his kitchen, brushed the cobwebs,
and told the egret to open all the doors.

SOWING

Angels are funny creatures because they flap
around and drop feathers in the most unlikely

places, then apologize for polluting the environment
but I know that secretly they consider their feathers

small gifts to fire the soul, quicken the
imagination and tickle the curious among us;

much like the words we drop here and there
or the dreams we spread around at noon

when the light is brightest, or even the love
we scatter - but angels know how to do it best

so we should carefully watch their journeys
to divine their ease, and their destination.

MR. BEE

Mr. Bee (I will presume the masculine in lieu of
a closer examination which I am not qualified to make)
alighted on my window this morning,

grabbed hold of the smooth surface, stayed
for a while, then died. He remained fixed there,
on the outside, never mind the breeze that rustled him

or the dust that dirtied his wearied eyes. No one
from his hive came to visit or plan obsequies,
like Uncle George who, we think, fell on a river of ice

and never wakened, was never noticed: a "Dies Irae"
never rang for him. Both had come to the end,
insides worn out and wanting only rest, searching

for the buzz and chant that would bring them home:
they could not hear its absence, but their own books
of life, in startlingly similar script, had assured them

that once they were pasted firmly to the earth,
like a taste of honey that is savored and planted in memory,
a new music would gambol, a kaleidoscope of prophecies

would weave themselves into a wild new tapestry
where the unicorn, freed from its pen, blesses his hunters,
and where weeds, in surprise, blossom into marigolds.

DAREDEVILS

The rain is just a whisper, hinting at stories I know
and one I can tell now if the elves stay quiet for a spell

he was an aerialist used to flying above the oohs and aahs
so not concerned about groundlings and their wide eyes

no, his realm was purer, designed to carve rapture and make
the air turn rectangles and circles even lift dreams high

but he saw a face tilted, once, noticed the fear and his legs
gave way; they say he was astonished as he fell straight down

but that's a sad one, I have other moments that need
deciphering, smaller moments that tell us why we look up

and search the daredevils for answers they see in our eyes.

THE LLAMA

I awoke this morning and found a llama
sitting at my desk, typing out an email;
the sky was still blue, on the lawn a few

crows pecked at acorns; the floor held my weight.
I'm not a submarine man, crawling along the bottom
to divine treasure or why it is there; I prefer

soup, crackers and pizza, so I did not consider
it unreasonable to ask him if it might be
prudent for him to leave. He said he was a student

of Ezekiel, that God had called him to spread
the good news that all would receive a new heart
and waves of joy would spring - he was messaging

the world. I asked him if he thought the world
would listen to a llama: "The strangest things
on earth," he said, "are God's delight and mirth,

they are the happiness God uses to send the Word."
This, of course, did not explain why he was in my house.
"Because you're strange, too." I thought it through

and tried to map a response, brushed away a bee
that sought my hand, then looked up and watched
the morning rise with music, children and butterflies.

DIFFERENCE

It's 3:32 p.m.
and I haven't produced
a single tear.

It's now 3:33: nothing.
I could journal this
forever and wind up

the same: waiting for
yesterday's event
to catch up.

The smallest flea
reacts immediately;
I suppose elephants

do, too, so I wonder:
is that the difference,
finally? That the stones

have to be gathered
slowly, the roses planted
and elms dug in

till they form a shrine
we can rest in. Time
is a prison guard for us

while for the leopard
watching in the dark
it is always now.

STAR

A star fell
at my feet
the other day,

a fledgling
lost in its circuit;
I looked to see

If anyone
was watching,
bent down

and petted it;
they're temperamental,
and their history

gives them
the right
of refusal,

so gently
I held it;
as night fell,

it shone —
my sign
to throw it high;

it was grateful.

TERESA'S SPARROW

This morning a sparrow flew in
and stood on my balcony, hesitated,
stepped closer and peeped in
at my reading of St. Teresa;

head skewed and eyes
blinking, as if listening to other
voices, searching another prize,
he seemed properly nonchalant,

but he noted - I think - with delight,
that Teresa floundered and fought
and prayed with startling sight
into the honor we owe to the God

who tackles us into life and shoves
us into prayer; stepping closer,
he dared the threshold, and since love
is the reason, I spread the page

for his perusal: what joy I noted
in his feathers as he pecked at the words:
but did he find a mystery coded
specially there for him

or was it a crumb I had dropped
from my morning snack? When finished,
he nodded winsomely and hopped
away. I was grateful for his attention.

EPILOGUE

THE RIGHT TAXI

I

"Are you ready?" she asked. I was not ready
for her: black fingernails shone
off the bright screen and her spider smile
promised exactly what it could give. I sat there
in easy darkness with a silver beam
over my head, watching memory
locked in black and white images
that offered no conclusion. She smiled
invitingly, knew my heart's sore.

II

Outside, rain slanted
and taxis looked for home;
the day kept its grimness
in a tight fist and waited,
silently, for my exit.

III

We tend to look for poetry (I thought)
and wind up pasted on plastic
when what causes true pain
is the poetry in our hands - a primeval force
not remembered and not fought for
but sensed: no beam of light

pointing the way is needed: the elf
inside has learned his wisdom before.

IV

Before leaving, I watched animals
in two dimensions jump over rocks,
insects skitter around, ghosts
smile, saints find their place;
watched black lace and waltzes
(knew a quiet race in my blood).
Those flashing images helped me decode
a journey I had begun and wanted
to continue. So I walked out the door.

V

Poetry is like grace: it's there
without petition, but you still must ask,
you must ride the right taxi.
So I stood on the corner, with rain slanting
to see my face, and put out my hand.

Made in the USA
San Bernardino, CA
12 January 2016